Every Single
Woman's Devotional

*30 Days of Strategic Prayer to Change
Your Life*

Nia Irvin-Smith

Copyright © 2016 Nia Irvin-Smith

To contact the author visit www.whileyouwait.org

Unless otherwise indicated, all scripture quotations are from the New King James Version ®. Copyright © 1982 by Thomas Nelson, Inc. Used by permission. All rights reserved.

Book Cover Designed By: The Creative Vue

ISBN-13: 978-1534803510

Dedication

To every woman seeking purpose, power and the
promises of God to change their life.

Introduction

God gave me the title of this devotional as a double entendre, or a phrase that's open to two interpretations. You can either read it as a devotional for single women or a devotional for every woman. That same ambiguity speaks to what I believe He wanted for this devotional's purpose. God wanted every woman, no matter what stage in life, to be able to seek Him each day about topics that relate directly to her. God wanted every woman, no matter what place spiritually, to come out of this with new insight and a deeper desire for intimacy with Him. So whether you have an established prayer time and this devotional will supplement it, or you're working on getting to that place and this devotional is a start, I want you to know that I wrote this for you.

Take the time to read each passage, pray each prayer and study each scripture. Every topic was prayerfully chosen, written and ordered to allow the Holy Spirit to do an inner work in you every day until you reach the completion. Ultimately, my prayer as the author is that this book is just a starting point. That you will begin to study out these subjects and not just say the prayers written here but make them personal to you. So as you commit to this time of study and prayer, be in expectation for the Lord to move in your life like never before. I believe and stand in agreement that by the time you end these 30 days, the Holy Spirit will have changed your life from the inside out.

Day 1

Spiritual Growth

As newborn babes, desire the pure milk of the word, that you may grow thereby, – 1 Peter 2:2

Every human being is fighting an internal battle, the war between your flesh and your spirit. Your spirit desires to do what is pleasing to God but the flesh wants to do the opposite. Winning this daily battle to honor God requires feeding your Spirit man, causing it to grow in strength beyond the will of the flesh. But if the things we take in everyday like TV, music, conversation, etc. constantly feed the flesh, it is bound to win. We are required to grow spiritually but just like in the natural, this is impossible without food. God has made that food available to us through His Word, but it's our responsibility to come to the table and eat. Take a moment and answer this question honestly, do you desire the Word of God? If you find yourself struggling with your desire for the Word, remember whatever you feed will grow. Make small goals of spending time with God and as your Spirit is fed, your desire for Him will grow.

Prayer: God, I give You glory for Your Word. Forgive me for any time I failed in keeping my commitment to You and placed You below Your rightful place in my life. Lord, I ask that You ignite a flame in me that burns for You. Help me to grow in revelation of the Word, allowing me to see and understand even more of who You are and who You have called me to be. I declare this day that I rededicate myself to time in Your presence and studying Your Word. Holy Spirit, as I spend time with You, open up my understanding and allow the Word to come alive to me like never before. In Jesus' Name, Amen.

Scriptures to meditate on:
Matthew 5:6
2 Timothy 2:15
Hebrews 4:12

Day 2

Hearing God's Voice

My sheep hear My voice, and I know them, and they follow Me. – John 10:27

One of the marks of an intimate relationship with God is knowing His voice, but a perspective clouded with doubt will hinder your ability to correctly discern His voice from others. The doubt is erased as we spend time in His presence and come to know what His voice sounds like. He often speaks through scripture but sometimes through dreams, people or whatever other way He can get through to you. Most of the time we don't hear God not because He's not speaking, but because we're too distracted to be able to hear what He's saying. We also need to read the Word so that the Holy Spirit has something to speak to us through. Everyday you read the Word is like adding scripture files to your memory. The Holy Spirit can

3

then speak to you by bringing back to your remembrance the scriptures that fit the different situations that arise. During your time with God, make sure that you are not just having a one-way conversation, spend time in the Word and leave room for God to speak to you also.

Prayer: Lord, I thank you that you are the true and living God. And because you are living and active, I can expect to hear your voice each and every day. God I invite you into my day to speak to me however you choose. I declare that my spiritual ears are open to hear from you and my heart is ready to receive whatever you have to say to me. I pray that as I spend time with you I learn to recognize your voice and gain confidence in our relationship. Help me learn how to quiet my Spirit and remove the distractions that busy my mind and keep me from hearing you. In Jesus' Name, Amen.

Scriptures to meditate on:
John 16:13-14
Hebrews 3:7-12

Day 3

Sensitivity to the Holy Spirit

But the Helper, the Holy Spirit, whom the Father will send in My name, He will teach you all things, and bring to your remembrance all things that I said to you. – John 14:26

Success in the Christian walk is impossible without the Holy Spirit. The Holy Spirit is so important that Jesus said it was better for us if He left because then He would send the Holy Spirit. Though the Holy Spirit is with us, we are often ignorant of the way He operates. The key to a healthy relationship with the Holy Spirit is sensitivity. Yes He speaks to us but there are also a lot of times the Holy Spirit communicates through prompts and nudges. That uneasy feeling that something isn't right or that peace you feel when you know you're doing the right thing. Those incidents are not just coincidences; they are God's way of speaking to you at that moment. While you're praying for the

Lord to speak to you about a matter, are you also being mindful of His nonverbal methods of communication? Instead of always seeking an outside voice, be more sensitive to the One within. Make sure He has His rightful place in your life so that He can be the helper the Lord sent Him to be.

Prayer: Lord, I ask Your forgiveness for ignoring the Helper you sent for me. As I grow in You and in Your Word, open my understanding and relationship with the Holy Spirit. As I make the conscious decision to be more aware of your promptings, I pray for an increase in my ability to quickly recognize and respond to the Holy Spirit. In the prayers I have before You, where I have asked You to speak to me, I will remain open to both Your voice and the other ways you can communicate with me. Remove anything that causes me to lose my sensitivity to Your Spirit and sharpen my spiritual ears to hear and eyes to see. I will no longer ignore the Spirit but instead will aim to be available to Him at all times. In Jesus' Name, Amen.

Scriptures to meditate on:
1 Thessalonians 5:19
Hebrews 12:7-11

Day 4

Purpose

For if you remain completely silent at this time, relief and deliverance will arise for the Jews from another place, but you and your father's house will perish. Yet who knows whether you have come to the kingdom for such a time as this?" –
Esther 4:14

Before you were ever a thought in the Earth, God loved you and ordained you to be a part of His eternal plan for mankind. His thoughts of you were full of intention; there was no one else that could do what He put you here to do. Unfortunately, over the course of time and the hustle and bustle of life, the world has shrunken our life's purpose into a pursuit of money, marriage, children and fame. But on the contrary, your purpose is not for you, but for God's glory and to evangelize the Kingdom of God. So what can you do today to intentionally

7

seek your REAL purpose? Pray for that coworker? Encourage that friend? Share Christ with your family members? Your purpose goes beyond a pulpit or a stage; it's the daily decisions you make to honor God. The small things you do, with a heart to please God, have the capacity to change someone's life forever. Make it a point to be aware of every opportunity to show forth God's glory, both big and small.

Prayer: Father God, I thank you for creating me with a unique purpose in Your kingdom. Today, I ask for revelation and direction concerning that purpose. Make it known to me, exactly why You placed me on this Earth so that I can pursue my purpose with clarity. Lord I pray for a divine encounter with You that will confirm my destiny. Let every gift and talent You've placed within me be recognized and sharpened in this season of my life. As I exercise my faith and serve in the kingdom, I thank You that my gift will make room for me and lives will be changed for Your glory. In Jesus' Name, Amen.

Scriptures to meditate on:
Jeremiah 1:5
Psalm 139:13-16
Ephesians 2:10

Day 5

Purity

For this is the will of God, your sanctification: that you should abstain from sexual immorality; 4 that each of you should know how to possess his own vessel in sanctification and honor, - 1 Thessalonians 4:3-4

For most people, the first thing that comes to mind in regards to purity is the physical. While physical purity is important, real purity is impossible without understanding that it is a result of the condition of your heart, not just your body. There are many people who live life physically pure but with impure hearts and minds, like the cup Jesus spoke of in Luke 11 who's exterior appeared clean while the inside was filled with dirt. Whether you are single or married, examine the condition of your heart, mind and then body. Your eyes and ears are gates to your soul, gates that affect your ability to maintain the vessel God has given you with honor. Be conscious of what you are allowing past your gates and whether it is feeding your flesh or your spirit. The will of God is your sanctification, to be set apart and able to be used for God's purpose. When God comes searching for a pure heart to work through, will He be able to use you?

Prayer: Lord, today I make the commitment to submit my whole self to You. I will guard my ears, eyes and heart from anything that would taint my ability to hear and see You clearly. Holy Spirit, show me the areas in which I need to be more aware of the desensitizing of my heart towards sin. As I seek to walk in complete purity, I declare no shame or guilt connected to my purity will hinder me from boldly approaching the throne of grace. Each day I receive the power to walk with a clear conscience as the water of Your Word washes me clean from all impurity. God I thank You for Your forgiveness and grace that gives me the strength to be in this world but not of it. In Jesus' Name, Amen.

Scriptures to meditate on:
Hebrews 10:22
Romans 12:2
Hebrews 4:15-16

Day 6

Thought Life

For "who has known the mind of the Lord that he may instruct Him?" But we have the mind of Christ. – 1 Corinthians 2:16

Your mind is a powerful and fascinating force. It is where we win or lose the battle we are waging with the enemy and our flesh everyday because it is the source of both our actions and our words. The most important thing to remember in that battle is that we are in control of our minds. Often we let our mind dictate how we feel, what we say, and what we do, but that's not the way it's meant to be. We were made to be led by the Spirit. You have to come to the realization that you have been given the mind of Christ. Anything contrary to the Word of God does not belong there and is the result of an opportunity you gave the enemy to impact your thought life; usually by not properly guarding your

11

eyes and ears. Today, make a commitment to be more aware of your thoughts. Make sure they line up with the Word of God so that you can successfully walk in faith.

Prayer: Lord right now I take authority over my thought life. I will guard my mind and not allow the enemy to have any mastery in my thoughts. I recognize that You have given me the power to bring every one of my thoughts into the obedience of Christ. I cast down every negative, defeated thought pattern and declare that Your Word renews my mind. My thoughts of myself, my life and others line up with the Word of God and nothing else. I have the mind of Christ; therefore I will think on things that are good, pure and true. Help me continue to shape my thought life into one that brings forth the good fruit of actions and words that are pleasing to You. In Jesus' Name, Amen.

Scriptures to meditate on:
Philippians 4:8
2 Corinthians 10:4-5
Ephesians 4:21-24

Day 7

Healing

He heals the brokenhearted and binds up their
wounds. - Psalm 147:3

Most airlines have a limit on the weight of the bags
a passenger can bring on a flight. They created
these rules because the plane has to maintain a
center of gravity so that it can take off, turn, and
land properly. The weight of the baggage literally
impacts the plane's ability to reach its destination
safely and on time and it is the same with us on this
journey of life. We carry hurt around like baggage.
Every negative word, the sting of rejection, the
emptiness of abandonment and pain of
disappointment are all pieces of baggage, weighing
us down and hindering us from moving to our
destination. Jesus endured all those things and more
so that we wouldn't have to be held back by their
weight. He offers to not only take on our burdens

for us but to heal us from any negative effects they may have left behind; whether it's just a wound or a broken heart. Every ounce of healing we could ever need was accomplished on the Cross. Release the heaviness of dealing with life on your own because Jesus died so you wouldn't have to. Give it over to God and leave it there.

Prayer: Father I pray today for your healing. Physically, mentally, and emotionally I receive your healing power that makes all things new. God I know that you are the potter and I am the clay, so mold and shape me in whatever way is needed. Every broken place within me is completely healed because of Your grace. I thank You for sending Jesus to endure hurt and pain on the cross so I would not have to. From this day forward, I will not carry the weight of any of the things Jesus has already taken from me through His death, burial and resurrection. You are the healer and I believe that nothing can separate me from You. In Jesus' Name, Amen.

Scriptures to meditate on:
3 John 1:2
Luke 8:40-48

Day 8

Wholeness

For in Him dwells all the fullness of the Godhead bodily; [10] *and you are complete in Him, who is the head of all principality and power. – Colossians 2:9-10*

The moment God created you, you were complete. You didn't need a college degree, a spouse, a certain job or a child...you weren't lacking anything. And then you were born, and the enemy launched a full out attack on your wholeness. His plan was to create as many thoughts of inadequacy in your life as possible; to create so many holes in your mind and emotions that you can't see the true glory of the person God created you to be. Things like the fear of abandonment or insecurity become voids. All voids that we will fill with things like drugs, alcohol, promiscuity and even food if we don't have a proper relationship with God. But no matter where you may feel inadequate or unfit, as a mother, as a wife, as a friend or anything else, you are complete in Christ. You were made for this. In Him there is nothing missing or broken and He is the One who lives inside of you. God is the only one who can fill those voids and make you whole, invite Him in so He can do just that.

Prayer: God I thank you that every empty place in me is filled by You. I am both healed and whole. I am not looking for anything outside of myself to make me feel complete; You completed me the day you created me in my mother's womb. You are the author and the finisher of my faith. I declare that nothing is missing or lacking in my life. Whether I am married or single, childless or mother of many, a new Believer or mature Christian, I have everything I need to be who You have called me to be. Fill me up so that I overflow with You in everything that I think, say and do. In Jesus' Name, Amen.

Scriptures to meditate on:
1 Peter 5:10-11
1 Thessalonians 5:23-24

Day 9

Grace

But by the grace of God I am what I am, and His grace towards me was not in vain; but I labored more abundantly than they all, yet not I, but the grace of God which was with me. – 1 Corinthians 15:10

Women wear many hats, a lot of them having to be worn at the same time. We're daughters, sisters, mothers, wives, friends and countless other roles. We are expected to be everything to everybody at all times. While all of these roles should be fulfilling, they can become very overwhelming when we try to do them in our own strength instead of operating through grace. We are naturally inclined to want to earn rewards so it's hard to accept that God has already freely given us all things, including grace. We don't have to do anything for Him to love us and bless us; it's a part of His grace or favor towards us. The pressure of trying to please God and please people is one you don't have to live under. Wherever you feel overwhelmed or stressed, accept God's grace to accomplish what needs to be done. He is waiting for you to stop trying to do everything on your own. Grace is available to help you navigate all that you need to do and be in your life and all you have to do is ask.

Prayer: Lord, thank You for Your grace. Your grace that empowers, Your grace that strengthens and Your grace that makes all Your sufficiency available to me. I give up trying to earn Your love or live a life that is holy through the flesh. I recognize that it is only by Your grace that I can live the life I am called to live. I will stop trying to do and be everything to everybody and seek to find the balance where I can operate in my place of grace. I am free from the burden of trying to do things in my own strength and now I receive the grace that enables me to do all things through Christ. Show me how to walk confidently in this grace, each and every day. In Jesus' Name, Amen.

Scriptures to meditate on:
Ephesians 2:8-9
2 Corinthians 9:8

Day 10

Emotional Maturity

So then, my beloved brethren, let every man be swift to hear, slow to speak, slow to wrath; [20] for the wrath of man does not produce the righteousness of God. – James 1:19-20

The thermostat and the thermometer are both used for temperature but they are very different. The thermometer reflects the current temperature of the environment but the thermostat is used to change the temperature to what is desired. In life, we have the option to be a thermostat or a thermometer. We can allow circumstances to dictate our attitude and actions, or we can allow our attitudes and actions to reflect the light of Christ regardless of the situation. Emotional maturity is the ability to handle everything life throws at you with poise. When you are pressed from every side do you cave in, or do you turn to God who promises to be your refuge?

When you're angry do you act out of character or seek peace to diffuse the situation? Search your heart for the root of anything that may cause you to reflect something other than Christ in your behavior and emotions and release them to God today in prayer.

"Circumstances don't create character; they reveal character." – Zig Ziglar

Prayer: Lord, today I submit my emotions to You. I declare that although I have emotions, I will not allow my emotions to have me. God I thank You for discipline and self-control that allow me to face the different circumstances in life with grace. I release the root of all negative emotions and impulsive behavior, including unforgiveness, disappointment, bitterness, pain and any other emotional trauma. I bring every emotional response into the obedience of Christ and when I am angry I will not sin by thought, word or action. I ask for Your help in recognizing all emotional trigger points and stumbling blocks that need to be covered in prayer. In Jesus' Name, Amen.

Scriptures to meditate on:
Ephesians 4:26-27
Proverb 29:11

Day 11

Peace

Peace I leave with you, My peace I give to you; not as the world gives do I give to you. Let not your heart be troubled, neither let it be afraid. – John 14:27

Each day is filled with invitations. Invitations wrapped in the daily occurrences of life. Invitations to get angry, invitations to be overwhelmed, invitations to be discouraged, invitations to be sad, etc. Believe it or not, we have the choice of which invitations we will accept. We don't have to go searching for the peace we need to combat these invitations; the Word says Jesus has already given it to us. He then tells us that if our heart is troubled or afraid, it's because we LET it be. Not only do we need to guard our peace but we also need to actually use the peace that we already have. So the question then becomes, what are you allowing to take your peace away? Today, instead of asking God for more peace, make a decision to take the responsibility of rejecting the invitations of all the things that wish to take the peace you already have away from you. Make peace your only option so that the Spirit of God can move in your life freely without disruption.

Prayer: Father God, thank You for providing Your children with peace. Help me to see and understand areas where I can do better in guarding the peace You have already given to me. I declare peace in every situation in my life and speak calm to any emotions or thought patterns that cause chaos or confusion in my inner man. I look first to You in times of tribulation and submit every one of my concerns to You; trusting that You will perfect them according to Your will. Thank You Lord that the peace of God guards my heart and mind from anything or anyone that wishes to disrupt the flow of Your Spirit in my life. In Jesus' Name, Amen.

Scriptures to meditate on:
Psalm 29:11
Isaiah 26:3
John 16:33

Day 12

Joy

You will show me the path of life; In Your presence is fullness of joy; At Your right hand are pleasures forevermore. – Psalm 16:11

What is joy to you? For most people, the definition of joy is happiness. They use the words interchangeably like they are one and the same. I believe the opposite of this is true. Joy is not an emotion like happiness; it's an attitude. Joy is Paul and Silas singing and praying in the midst of being locked in a prison. Joy is Joseph determining that in spite of his trials, everything the devil meant for evil, God would turn into good. Joy is a confidence so strong in God that your emotions are untouched by your circumstances. You choose joy; it doesn't just happen periodically like an emotion. And the foundation of joy is peace. Peace that knows in your innermost being that God is and always will be in control. That assurance is the forerunner to accessing the joy that is always available in God's presence. Choose to access joy by getting into God's presence today through worship, prayer and the Word.

Prayer: Lord, I thank You for the understanding that You are the source of all of my joy. I recognize that it is only in You that I can experience what real joy is. I will never again allow the enemy to steal the confidence in You that allows me to have joy regardless of the circumstance. I declare that You are the Lord of my life and that peace makes my joy unshakable. Because of this joy, I declare that I am a light to those around me and I can provide comfort to them in their times of need. In my own times of sadness or despair, I will remember to get out of my emotions and into Your presence. In Jesus' Name, Amen.

Scriptures to meditate on:
Psalm 126:5
James 1:2-3
Nehemiah 8:10

Day 13

Wisdom

If any of you lacks wisdom, let him ask of God, who gives to all liberally and without reproach, and it will be given to him. – James 1:5

What would your life be like if you had access to God's wisdom every single day? What if you were always able to make the right decisions, succeed in whatever you put your hand to and avoid life's pitfalls? God's wisdom can make that a reality and He made it so that all we have to do to get it is ask. Ask God how to have healthy relationships and how to be successful at work. Ask God how to budget your money and use your time effectively. No question is too big or too small. God wants to be invited into your whole life, including your everyday affairs. He longs to give you insight and understanding so that you can successfully navigate each day, but He can only do so when you acknowledge that you need it by asking. What situations are you dealing with that you haven't taken the time to ask God about? Use your prayer time today to simply ask for wisdom wherever you feel you need it and have faith that He will hear you and grant your petition.

Prayer: Heavenly Father, today I ask for wisdom. Wisdom to govern my life's affairs in a way that is pleasing to You and advances Your purpose in my life. Holy Spirit, right now I receive your instruction for every situation where I feel confused or stuck. Because even when I don't know what to do, I am connected to the One who does. Instead of seeking friends and family first, I will listen intently for Your voice that is meant to lead and guide me into all truth. Today I clear my heart of all of the world's wisdom and make room for the wisdom that comes from above. Help me to govern my life according to Your righteousness and not my own. In Jesus' Name, Amen.

Scriptures to meditate on:
Proverbs 4:7
Proverbs 2:6-7
James 3:16-17

Day 14

Discernment

But solid food belongs to those who are of full age, that is, those who by reason of use have their senses exercised to discern both good and evil. –
Hebrews 5:14

Have you ever been in a situation where you trusted someone and it turned out negatively? Or made a bad decision that could've easily been avoided? In these cases it would have helped to have spiritual discernment, or the ability to judge something correctly. As Believers, we need discernment because our adversary is the father of lies. He deceived Eve and continues to do the same thing to people today. That is his weapon of choice and we can't be ignorant of the enemy's devices. The discernment we need, so that we are not tricked, comes from the Holy Spirit. It's something we have to learn to use by exercising our spiritual senses. We do this by living a life where we are truly submitted to the Holy Spirit's leading. It is through Him that we can see what's beyond human sight. What looks good on the outside is not always beneficial in the end. In addition to the Holy Spirit, test everything against the Word. Anything God sends will not contradict His Word. From now on, before making any decisions, ask God for discernment. It could be the difference between success and failure.

Prayer: Lord, today I pray for an increase in my discernment. As I mature in my relationship with You, I ask that you improve my ability to see beyond what my eyes can see and into the spiritual elements that are behind the natural occurrences. As I exercise discernment, reveal to me strategic plans that I can use to war effectively in prayer against the enemy's plans for my life and those around me. I know that this battle cannot be won by flesh and blood so I invite Your Spirit in to guide me in the right direction. Holy Spirit, I will listen for your voice of wisdom so that I can recognize the Truth that comes from You versus the deception that comes from the enemy. In Jesus' Name, Amen.

Scriptures to meditate on:
1 John 4:1-3
1 Peter 5:8

Day 15

Focus

And this I say for your own profit, not that I may put a leash on you, but for what is proper, and that you may serve the Lord without distraction. – 1 Corinthians 7:35

Everyone and everything in your life is on assignment, whether that assignment is good or bad. All things can be categorized into what God has sent to bring something to your life or what the enemy has sent to take something away. And oftentimes what the enemy is trying to take away is your focus. Our sole purpose is for God to be glorified and anything that takes away from that is a distraction. While you're distracted, you're idle. You're not moving backwards but you're not moving forward either. We would easily be able to guard against this distraction if the damage came all at once but it doesn't happen that way. It's a slow erosion. You look up a week, a month, a year later and realize you haven't achieved your goals or grown in your walk with God and all because you've been...busy. Take an assessment of your life and anything that's just a distraction has to go. It can be a person, an activity or anything that's unnecessarily consuming your time. Take this opportunity to refocus and get back on track to serving the Lord without distraction.

Prayer: Father God, I repent for any time I've spent being distracted from serving You. I declare this day that my focus is completely on You. As I assess my life, help me to discern the things and people that are hindering me in any way from being able to grow and move forward in my walk with You. Show me where to focus my attention and energy so that I can advance Your Kingdom without wasting time on unnecessary tasks. I claim victory over every distraction the enemy meant for evil in my life and declare that from now on I will intentionally guard my heart and mind from anything that does not glorify You. In Jesus' Name, Amen.

Scriptures to meditate on:
Luke 10:38-42
Proverbs 4:25-27
Luke 8:11-15

Obedience

Then He said to them all, "If anyone desires to come after Me, let him deny himself, and take up his cross daily, and follow Me. – Luke 9:23

When God formed the Garden of Eden, He could have very well made all the trees good and given Adam and Eve no choice but to do what was right. So why didn't He? Instead, God chose to give them the opportunity to choose. There is only real obedience when you have options, not when you have no other choice. Adam and Eve had to choose to serve God, they were granted freedom of choice. And ever since the tree of the knowledge of good and evil was created, every other person has been given that same freedom. Every day you have the option to choose God or this world. And every decision you make is a testimony of which one you have chosen. Today, keep in mind the need to always make Godly decisions. Your obedience will always be tested. If you are really a follower of Christ, no matter what the consequences or rewards, you will always choose God.

Prayer: Lord, I thank You for empowering me through the Holy Spirit to be able to choose to be obedient to You. I submit my whole life to You and ask that You would lead me so that all my choices are a reflection of my faith in You. God I thank you that you have already promised to honor those who honor You so I am able to trust You no matter what decisions I have to face. Everyday I will exercise my power to choose to serve You with my whole heart. My obedience is a testament of my love for You. Wherever You lead me God, I will follow and whatever You tell me to do, I will do it. All for your glory. In Jesus' Name, Amen.

Scriptures to meditate on:
Isaiah 1:19
1 Peter 1:13-16
Joshua 24:14-15

Day 17

Patience

But let patience have its perfect work, that you may be perfect and complete, lacking nothing. - James 1:4

Life is full of waiting. You wait in the doctor's office, you wait in line at the grocery store, and you even wait in the drive-thru line at your favorite fast food place. We literally have to wait for something every day, so why do we have such a problem with patience when it comes to the things of God? Understand that there are only 2 reasons God is making you wait. Either He is preparing you for the promise or He is preparing the promise for you. Sometimes we are not ready for what we've asked God for and other times He needs to make some other shifts and changes as He orchestrates the lives of millions of people just like you. Your ability to be patient is a direct reflection of how much you trust God. Do you really believe that God's timing is perfect and He wouldn't withhold anything good thing from you? Instead of complaining or rushing God, be reminded that to everything there is a season and God has already purposed the right time for you to receive whatever it is you are asking Him for. All you have to do is wait.

Prayer: Father God, thank You for already providing me with everything I need to be victorious in life. As I practice waiting on You, I thank You that the fruit of patience grows within me. For every moment I need to wait on You, I pray that You would remind me of Your love towards me and Your plan to bring me good and not harm. I recognize that every waiting period is an opportunity to grow in faith and perseverance. I choose to trust You without complaint or anxiety, having full faith that You hear my prayers and they have been answered. I submit to the process as You prepare the promise for me and I am willing to wait so that I am ready when the promise comes. In Jesus' Name, Amen.

Scriptures to meditate on:
James 1:2-3
Philippians 4:6-7
2 Peter 3:9

Day 18

Self-Image

You did not choose Me, but I chose you and
appointed you that you should go and bear fruit,
and that your fruit should remain, that whatever
you ask the Father in My name He may give you. –
John 15:16

Sometimes we block our own blessings. Not by
being disobedient or sinning, but simply because
deep down we feel we don't deserve them. The
magnitude to which we are able to receive from
God in our life is based upon our understanding of
who we are in Christ. You are worthy, you are
valuable and you deserve the best. Not because of
how hard you worked or how well you did, but
simply because of the grace of Jesus. We couldn't
earn salvation but he freely gave it to us, and since
He did, who are we to go back and say what we
don't deserve? Condition your mind to see yourself
the way God sees you. God loves you so much,

more than your parents, a spouse, or even your best friend. He loves you unconditionally, passionately and eternally. He doesn't even see your flaws; to Him you are simply beautiful. Don't settle for less than you deserve or reject the goodness He is sending your way. If you don't love yourself you will always attract things and people that don't love you either. Your relationship with yourself sets the standard for everything else in your life, so set the standard high.

Prayer: Lord, I praise You and thank You for being the Creator of life. Thank You for choosing me before I chose You. Thank You for loving me even before I loved You. Forgive me for any time I blocked your blessings by my own feelings of low self-esteem or self-pity. Help me to see myself the way You see me and embrace my flaws as the ways You have made me unique. Remind me of Your love for me and expand the capacity of my heart and mind to receive even more of Your love. Let this new understanding of Your love for me also shape my hope and expectations to be greater than they've ever been before. In Jesus' Name, Amen.

Scriptures to meditate on:
Psalm 139:14
1 Peter 2:9

Day 19

Unconditional Love

And above all things have fervent love for one another, for "love will cover a multitude of sins." –
1 Peter 4:8

In life, even more so now with social media, we have grown very callused. Our thoughts are towards the best interest of ourselves and we don't have time to contribute to someone else's life unless it directly benefits us in some way. But in John 13, the characteristic Jesus said that His followers should be known by is love. And not just love towards Him, but the love we have for one another. So then why do we hold people to these impossible standards to deserve our love while at the same time crying out for people to love us, flaws and all? The easiest way to receive love is to give it. Constantly sow seeds of compassion and graciousness and those same things will come back to you. Love covers, love forgives, love endures and most of all it doesn't expect anything in return. You are called to be an extension of God's hand and heart in this Earth. Find something nice to say or do for someone today, you never know what kind of impact it will have.

Prayer: Lord, today I pray for a heart like Yours. I want to love people with the same love that You have shown to me. Help me to look beyond their imperfections and see every person as Your child whom You love just like You love me. Remove the hypocrisy and pride that causes me to see others differently than what You see them. I give past hurts and disappointments that cause me to love with conditions over to You and decide today to walk in forgiveness. Let the light of Your love be apparent in every one of my words and actions so that people can see and experience You through me. In Jesus' Name, Amen.

Scriptures to meditate on:
1 Corinthians 13:1-13
1 John 4:7-12
John 15:12-13

Day 20

Friendship

The righteous should choose his friends carefully,
For the way of the wicked leads them astray. –
Proverb 12:26

Life is not an isolated experience. We are forced in every way to form relationships in order to reach our highest potential. Whether it is at church or on your job, you need friends. For such an important subject, it is not often one we pray about. We choose friends based on compatibility like being involved in the same organizations or liking the same things without ever considering the purpose of the relationship. Your life has the ability to either be enhanced or diminished by the people you choose to associate with, so choose your inner circle carefully. Life can be hard at times and God has created friendships as an extra source of both encouragement and enjoyment. Do your friends encourage you with the Word of God? Do they pray for you? Do they challenge you to be a better person? These are the characteristics of a Godly friend. Don't just search for one, be one.

Prayer: Lord, I pray right now for every relationship in my life. Reveal their purpose to me and show me who You have ordained to be in my life and who You have not. I pray that You would continue to send Godly people into my life who will help push me into my destiny and cause me to part ways with anyone who is holding me back. Give me both the discernment to recognize a Godly friend and the wisdom on how to be one. Help me to see areas in which I can serve my current friends and their purpose so that all of my relationships glorify You. In Jesus' Name, Amen.

Scriptures to meditate on:
Proverbs 27:17
Ecclesiastes 4:9-10

Day 21

Understanding

The eyes of your understanding being enlightened;
that you may know what is the hope of His calling,
what are the riches of the glory of His inheritance
in the saints, - Ephesians 1:18

Confusion is one of the greatest deterrents to a Believer's walk with Christ. Things are happening all around us and to us, some good and some bad, and the biggest question we would like to ask God is…why? Because if we knew why it would be easier to handle. If we knew why it would be simpler to understand. But sometimes there is no answer to the question "why?" that we will understand. We just have to depend on our knowledge of God's will. His will is simple; we are the ones that make it complicated. God's will is for all to be saved and come to the knowledge of the truth (1 Timothy 2:4). Being saved and coming to the knowledge of the truth are two different things.

Once you get saved, you are still on the journey to coming to know the fullness of the truth. Our understanding is opened to this truth piece-by-piece and moment-by-moment. Instead of being hindered by what you don't understand, pursue the truth through the light of the Word and the teaching of the Holy Spirit.

Prayer: Father God, I praise You today as the omniscient God. The one who sees all and knows all. I ask for You to open up the eyes of my understanding Lord. Free me from every area of wrong thinking that causes confusion or doubt in my life and take me to a new level in my walk with You. Cause me to know and comprehend more of Your truth. Shine Your light on areas of darkness within my understanding of Your will. God, I want a deeper revelation of who You are. A fresh revealing of You in all of Your glory, in ways I have never seen You before. And I pray for not only a deeper revelation but an ability to articulate this understanding so that I can be a light for Your people. In Jesus' Name, Amen.

Scriptures to meditate on:
Colossians 1:9-10
John 6:38-40
Ephesians 5:15-17

Day 22

Strength

Strength and honor are her clothing; She shall rejoice in time to come. – Proverb 31:25

One of the enemy's tactics against us as women is to skew the reality of who we are. We are so resilient and so tenacious that the only way to stop us is to make us think and feel the exact opposite. Satan bombards us with reminders of our failures and speaks to our insecurities so that we lose confidence in our God-given abilities. And he does all of this so that we don't expect to see God move when we pray and to achieve anything we put our minds to. Because if we did believe these things…we would be unstoppable. But woman, you are strong. Even in your most vulnerable state you are draped in strength and dignity. Clothing only your Heavenly Father could provide. Regardless of how you feel or what you see when you look in the mirror, don't let the enemy stop you today. Whatever you tried before that didn't work, try again. Whatever you feel you can't do, do it anyways. We are strong in the Lord; seek Him for strength.

Prayer: Heavenly Father, I pray today for renewed strength. Forgive me for ever looking over the strength You blessed me with as Your child. I thank you Lord that I am strong in You. For it is when I am weak that You are able to show Yourself strong in me. Holy Spirit, meet me where I am and have your way in my life. Areas where I've been broken down, I ask for You to rebuild. Areas where I'm shaky and uncertain, I ask for You to fortify them. Reshape my thinking so that I can magnify Your strength in me and not my weaknesses by myself. Give me the courage I need to try again and the hope I need to keep pressing towards the finish line. In Jesus' Name, Amen.

Scriptures to meditate on:
Philippians 4:13
Ephesians 6:10
2 Corinthians 12:9-10

Day 23

Endurance

*Therefore do not cast away your confidence, which
has great reward. For you have need of endurance,
so that after you have done the will of God, you
may receive the promise: - Hebrews 10:35-36*

Doing the right thing doesn't always have immediate rewards. It can even begin to look like those who are living outside of the will of God are doing better than those who are. But that's why the Word says we have need of endurance…lasting power. Life works in seasons. Every prayer, every kind word and good thing that you do is a seed planted in the ground. A lot of times we're expecting a harvest from a seed we either haven't planted or we just planted not that long ago. Yes miracles can happen, but most of the time you're going to have to endure the planting and growing seasons before you get to the harvest. Your reward for enduring is that you will receive the promise of God both now and in Heaven. Don't allow the passage of time to cause you to lose your confidence and dig up the seeds you have planted. Continue in prayer and hold fast to your faith, you will reap in due season if you don't lose heart (Galatians 6:9).

Prayer: Lord, I praise you for giving me strength so that through You I can endure until I reach my due season. I believe that every seed I have in the ground right now will not return empty but produce an abundant harvest. I reject the thought that anything I have given to You or done for You was in vain. You are not unjust to forget my labor of love, so I cast away all doubt, discouragement and unbelief and restore my faith in You. You are the source of the sustaining power I need to keep pressing towards the prize. And it is through that power that I will remain steadfast and immoveable continuing to do the good works You have called me to do. In Jesus' Name, Amen.

Scriptures to meditate on:
James 1:12
Hebrews 12:1-2
Hebrews 6:13-15

Day 24

Faith

Then He touched their eyes, saying, "According to your faith let it be to you." – Matthew 9:29

We find Jesus throughout the Bible telling people that what they received from Him was based on their faith. The woman with the issue of blood, the two blind men, and the centurion soldier all received their miracle from Jesus because of their faith. In essence, yes Jesus had the power, but it took their faith to access it. Your life's success is the sum total of what you have the capacity to believe God for, not what God will choose to do for you. In fact, the Word says that we are to live and walk BY faith. Why? Because God would never give us a life that doesn't require Him. When was the last time you believed God for something you knew only He could do? How often do you limit your prayer requests based on the fear of God not doing what you ask? Today, create a space for God in your life by stretching your faith capacity. Expand your vision and intensify your prayer time. Take the human limits off of God and access the miraculous with your faith.

Prayer: Father God, forgive me for limiting You with my own fear. My desire is to live a life of faith because I know without faith it is impossible to please You. I thank You that You have already provided everything I need and now I just need to access it. I declare that my faith is the bridge between where I am and where I want to be. Show me how to exercise my faith to connect to all the promises You have for me. I increase my expectation for You to supernaturally move in my life and I receive the courage to step out in faith and walk in it. In Jesus' Name, Amen.

Scriptures to meditate on:
Hebrews 11:6
2 Corinthians 5:7
Matthew 17:20

Day 25

Vision

Then the LORD *answered me and said: "Write the vision and make it plain on tablets, that he may run who reads it. – Habukkuk 2:2*

Vision is the graphic component of faith but it is not what you see with your physical eyes. Your physical sight sees things the way that they are, but vision see things the way God sees them. Vision is the bigger picture of your life and goals are the roadway to get you there, not the destination. A lot of us focus on having achievable objectives...finishing school, landing a good job, making it to a certain income level, etc. but what are you ultimately working towards and how does it fit into your life's purpose? You have to know where you are going before you can figure out how to get there. Take the time today to write out a vision for every area of your life and then make sure the goals you've set for yourself fit into that vision. However, don't make these plans without consulting the Lord. Often what we view for ourselves is much less than what God would and we need a vision built on faith. Commit your plans to the Lord and as you continue in faith, He will establish them (Proverbs 16:3).

Prayer: God, I pray today that You would show me the vision You have for every area of my life. Help me to see beyond my current circumstances and into what You see when You look at my life through the lens of hope. In my career, my family, my ministry, my health, my finances and my relationships, I declare that I will run with vision and supersede every goal set before me. I will not allow anything to discourage or distract me from seeing to it that my life is always fruitful, turning my vision into reality. Expand my thoughts of Your plan for me into a vision that is not just local but national and global; to impact the world with the love of Jesus through the opportunities You present to me both big and small. In Jesus' Name, Amen.

Scriptures to meditate on:
Proverbs 29:18
Philippians 3:13-14

Day 26

Trust

Trust in the LORD with all your heart, and lean not on your own understanding; - Proverbs 3:5

Abraham was 99 years old when God told him that Sarah, his 90-year-old wife, would bear him a son. In the moment, he laughed at the possibility of a couple their age producing a child, and yet we honor Abraham as the Father of faith. So, how did he get from unbelief to faith? Abraham trusted God. According to Romans 4:19, he trusted God by not considering the deadness of his own body or Sarah's womb. The opposite of trusting God is not unbelief, but rather placing your trust in the wrong thing. We can't take into consideration the natural circumstances when as Christians we are called to live a life governed by the supernatural. Abraham chose to place his trust in God's faithfulness. What will you choose to consider when it's time to trust

God's promises? Your own inadequacies, the current status of your bank account, the way that you feel? Place your trust in God, who is able to do all that He has promised. Real trust in God always starts with the impossible.

Prayer: Father God, I declare today that I trust You. I will not lean to my own understanding but instead consider Your kindness, goodness and faithfulness towards me. You are not a man that You should lie, therefore You are completely worthy of all of my trust. I will no longer consider my current circumstances; they are not a measure of Your ability. I rein in my thoughts and focus on the truth of Your Word. You are the same God yesterday, today and forever. The same faithfulness You showed Abraham, You will show towards me. I believe that You are fully capable of performing every promise You have made and I stand in expectancy to see that manifested in my life. In Jesus' Name, Amen.

Scriptures to meditate on:
Psalm 5:11
Psalm 18:30

Day 27

Contentment

*Not that I speak in regard to need, for I have
learned in whatever state I am, to be content: -
Philippians 4:11*

The most standout scriptures we have that were
directly about contentment came from the Apostle
Paul. He led a very tumultuous life after
experiencing his conversion to Christ, including
stints in prison and persecution. In spite of all of
this, he said he learned to be content. As he went
through the different trials, some common thread
between all of them had taught him something. I
believe that Paul's ability to be content was rooted
in gratefulness. He often wrote about how
unworthy and undeserving he was of God's grace
and yet he kept pressing on. Anything he had to
endure or even anything he gained paled in
comparison to what God had already done for him

in saving his soul. Have you ever stopped to thank God just for saving you? For the opportunity and the presence of mind to accept the salvation that many people will die without? Things and people will come and go but the saving power of Jesus is worth being thankful for. Make sure you always operate out of a place of gratefulness. It is from there that all the good things God has for you will flow.

Prayer: Heavenly Father, I want to tell You today that I am grateful that You saved me. You saved me not only from eternal separation from You but from having to go through this life without You. Forgive me for any time I operated out of self-entitlement and show me where I may have exalted temporal things above that which is eternal. Holy Spirit, help me to always remember all the things I have to be thankful for. My life in Christ is a prize I could have never earned. I commit to using my life as a gift back to You for all that You've done for me. You are a good God, a good Father and a good Shepherd and I will worship You forever. In Jesus' Name, Amen.

Scriptures to meditate on:
Ephesians 2:8
Romans 6:22-23

Day 28

Prosperity

And my God shall supply all your need according to His riches in glory by Christ Jesus. – Philippians 4:19

God's will is for you to prosper. Is that hard for you to believe? We are often fed this image of a God who wants us to barely get by in life, just in case abundance would cause us to trust in something other than Him. That kind of thinking creates a fear of prosperity instead of the assurance we should have because it's our right as children of God. God takes pleasure in our well-being, not our troubles. Prospering is not limited to finances. Jesus came so that we could be healed, made whole and set free from anything less than God's best. Don't wake up in the morning with negative thoughts. Confess that goodness and mercy will follow you all the days of your life. Set the course of your life on the expectation of prosperity and don't let anything discourage you. God's plan for you today, and every day, is good and not evil. As you seek Him, He has promised to do exceedingly, abundantly above anything you could ask or think and that's real prosperity.

Prayer: Father God, I thank You that You are my source and your supply is unlimited. Everything I need and everything I want comes from You. God I believe that Your plan for me is to prosper. I pray today that you download into me Your plan for my prosperity: in my finances, in my relationships, and in my health. Holy Spirit, teach me how to use what You've already given me to create wealth and success that will last a lifetime. Wellness, in every area of my life, is my portion and my right. I bind all lack in the name of Jesus. Lack of finances, lack of love, lack of health and all other forms of lack have no avenue to enter my life. Right now I receive Your wisdom, knowledge and understanding that are necessary to govern a life filled with abundance. In Jesus' Name, Amen.

Scriptures to meditate on:
Psalm 103:2-5
Psalm 35:27

Day 29

Divine Positioning

*The steps of a good man are ordered by
the LORD, and He delights in his way. – Psalm
37:23*

God is a divine orchestrator. He's in control of
millions of lives, all at the same time and yet still
wills for every one of our lives to be blessed. The
only thing standing between us and our next
season, breakthrough or blessing is timing and
positioning. Usually these things don't just happen
at a certain time but at a certain place, and that
place can be natural or spiritual. Once we learn
how to master waiting, we must also be submitted
to the Lord's guidance so that He can position us
mentally and physically to receive what He has for
us. Ruth never would've encountered God's favor
in the form of Boaz if she hadn't listened to
Naomi's instructions of where to be and when to be
there. God may need you to take some action in

order to cause you to cross paths with the answer to your prayers. Don't let laziness cause you to miss your blessing. He is leading you somewhere and the result is going to be good.

Prayer: Lord, today I reconfirm the decision to make You the leader of my life. Your hand is always on me, moving and shifting every element of my life so that all things work together for my good. I pray right now that You direct my path to the right places, at the right times and with the right people. Send divine connections that will help me move forward in my purpose and my walk with You. Lead me to people that need me and the gifts You have given me. Open my eyes to see where You have positioned me to be the answer to someone's prayer. Grant me the opportunity to be the blessing and not just receive it, so that You may be glorified. In Jesus' Name, Amen.

Scriptures to meditate on:
Proverbs 16:9
Book of Ruth

Day 30

Hope

And we know that all things work together for good to those who love God, to those who are the called according to His purpose. – Romans 8:28

The glory of serving a God so loving and kind is the ability to have hope. Hope is so important the Bible describes it as the anchor of our soul. It keeps us grounded when life's trials try to push us off into despair and discouragement. It provides us with the strength to get back up when we get knocked down. We have this hope that our lives are not in vain, that we were created with purpose on purpose and predestined for greatness. We have this hope that we will experience God's goodness both now and in eternity because even the bad that has happened will ultimately end up being for our good. Yes we have this hope, but now what we have to do is hold onto it. Through the ups and downs, joys and pains…hold on. And as you hold on, spread it to others. Spread hope to your family, hope to your friends, and hope to this world. Point them to Jesus, the author and finisher of our faith, because He is our hope and that is our duty.

Prayer: Father God, I want to thank You that You are our hope. As long as we are with You, we can always expect a good outcome. Though the exact events of the future are unknown, I put my trust in You; the One who knows everything. You hold my whole world in Your hands. I declare that everything that has happened in my life up until now is working together for my good. That each event was necessary to propel me towards my destiny and now I will begin to see Your purpose manifest in my life. I will not be held back by the past. You will never leave me or forsake me. As my mind is renewed by Your Word, so is my hope in You. In Jesus' Name, Amen.

Scriptures to meditate on:
2 Corinthians 4:16-18
Lamentations 3:24
Hebrews 6:17-19

Closing Prayer

Father, I give You glory for each day these last 30 days that I have been able to spend time with You using this devotional. Thank You for opening up my understanding, speaking to my heart and giving me a fresh revelation of who You are. I declare from this day forward, my life will never be the same. I have a better understanding of my purpose, Your plan for me and every promise I have access to as a woman of God. Because of this time spent with You, I thank You that I am firmly rooted, built up and established in my faith. Holy Spirit, whenever I need it, bring back to my remembrance every Scripture I have read and prayer I have prayed during this time. I thank You that they are all now written on my heart and nothing will ever take that away. As I continue to seek You with all my heart, build upon the new things I have learned and show me how to best run the race that has been set before me. In Jesus' Name, Amen.

Are you in a place where you feel like you are waiting on God to do something for you? Purchase your copy of Nia's book "While You Wait..." to learn life-changing principles about your journey to receiving God's promises and better understand the purpose behind your wait.

ORDER NOW!
www.whileyouwait.org

Made in the USA
Lexington, KY
06 May 2017